DATE DUE

FE 5 '90	C 8 '90		
FE 12 '90	C 11 '90		
FE 19 '90	C 18 '90		
R 5 '90	30 '90		
R 12 '90	02 '90		
MR 19 '90	DE 17 '90		
MR 27 '90	A 17 '9		
P 5 '90	A 28 '9		
D 12 '90	FE 7 '91		
Y 11 '90	FE 19 '9		
MY 14 '90	E 21 '9		
SE 27 '90	R 11 '91		

Si

        Silly rhymes

SILLY RHYMES

Chosen and illustrated
by Mik Brown

*An index of first lines and authors
is on page 32.*

WARWICK PRESS
New York/London/Toronto/Sydney
1988

For Toby, Jacob, Lucie, Theo and Zoe

The editor and publishers gratefully acknowledge
permission to reproduce the following copyright material:
Martin Honeysett: ''A hibernating hedgehog'' and ''Mrs Pig''
from *Animal Nonsense Rhymes* (Methuen). Reprinted by
permission of Methuen Children's Books. Laura E. Richards:
''Eletelephony'' from *Tirra Lirra: Rhymes Old and New.*
Copyright © 1932 by Laura E. Richards. Copyright ©
renewed 1960 by Hamilton Richards. Reprinted by
permission of Little Brown and Company.

Published in 1988 by Warwick Press,
387 Park Avenue South, New York, New York 10016.
First published in 1987 by Kingfisher Books Ltd.
This collection copyright © Mik Brown 1987.
Illustrations copyright © Mik Brown 1987.

Library of Congress Catalog Card No. 88-50130
ISBN 0-531-19047-1

Printed in Spain

If you should see a crocodile . . .

If you should see a crocodile
Don't take a stick and poke him;
Ignore the welcome of his smile,
Be careful not to stroke him.
For as he sleeps upon the Nile,
He thinner gets and thinner;
And whenever you meet a crocodile
He's ready for his dinner.

Anon

A sea serpent

A sea serpent saw a big tanker,
Bit a hole in her side and then sank her,
It swallowed the crew,
In a minute or two,
And then picked its teeth with the anchor.

Anon

A hibernating hedgehog

A hibernating hedgehog,
Woke up to greet the spring,
He'd set the alarm for half-past May,
But he hadn't heard it ring.
In fact he'd gone and overslept,
A silly thing to do,
Not only had he missed the spring,
He'd missed the summer too.

Martin Honeysett

5

Bengal

There was a young man of Bengal
Who went to a fancy dress ball;
He went just for fun
Dressed up as a bun
And a dog ate him up in the hall.

Anon

Kilkenny cats

There were once two cats of Kilkenny
Each thought there was one cat too many;
So they fought and they fit,
And they scratched and they bit,
Till, excepting their nails,
And the tips of their tails,
Instead of two cats, there weren't any.

Anon

ATISHOOO!

There was a young tiger

There was a young tiger at the zoo
Who discovered he kept catching flu.
He thought, in these breezes
It's no wonder I sneezes
I'll probably get bronchitis too.

Sarah Mills

I wish I were

I wish I were a little grub,
With whiskers on my tummy,
I'd climb into a honey pot
And get my tummy gummy.

Anon

Eletelephony

Once there was an elephant,
Who tried to use the telephant –
No! No! I mean an elephone
Who tried to use the telephone –
(Dear me, I am not certain quite
That even now I've got it right.)

Howe'er it was, he got his trunk
Entangled in the telephunk;
The more he tried to get it free,
The louder buzzed the telephee –
(I fear I'd better drop this song
Of elephop and telephong!)

Laura Richards

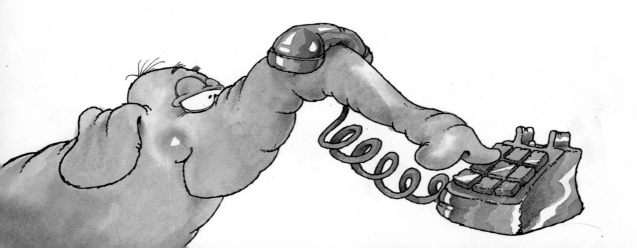

Algy

Algy met a bear
A bear met Algy
The bear grew bulgy
The bulge was Algy.

Anon

Fuzzy Wuzzy

Fuzzy Wuzzy was a bear,
Fuzzy Wuzzy had no hair,
Fuzzy Wuzzy wasn't fuzzy,
Was he?

Anon

The horny goloch

The horny goloch
Is an awesome beast
Soople and scaly
It has two hands
And a hantle of feet
And a forkie tailie

Anon

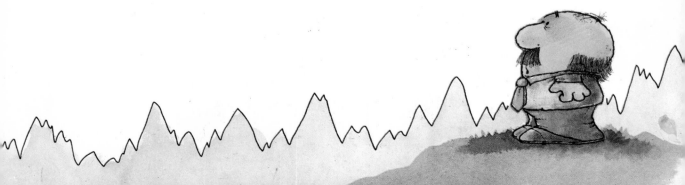

I don't suppose

I don't suppose a lobster knows,
The proper way to blow its nose,
Or else perhaps beneath the seas,
It had no need to sniff and sneeze.

Anon

A gorilla

A gorilla once visited Spain,
And said crossly, "I'll not come again,
A land full of farmers
Who can't grow bananas
And it's true what they say about rain."

Sarah Mills

The boy stood on the burning deck

The boy stood on the burning deck
His feet began to blister
The flames leapt up
And burned his pants
So now he wears his sister's.

Anon

Little Miss Muffet

Little Miss Muffet,
Sat on a tuffet,
Eating her Irish stew;
There came a big spider
Who sat down beside her
And she ate him up, too, with the stew.

Anon

I'd like to be an octopus

I'd like to be an octopus,
With arms on every corner,
I'd scare my grannie close to death;
I wouldn't even warn her.

John Paton

I eat my peas with honey

I eat my peas with honey,
I've done it all my life,
It makes the peas taste funny,
But it keeps them on the knife.

Anon

21

Kinga the kanga

Kinga the kanga,
And Ricky the roo,
Bounced up and down—
That's what kangaroos do.
Kanga could jump
Not just one foot but two,
And deep in her pouch,
Ricky played peekaboo.

Sarah Mills

Mrs. Pig

Mrs. Pig,
Was not very big,
Her husband even smaller.
From morning till evening,
They'd hang from the ceiling,
In the hope that they'd make themselves taller.

Martin Honeysett

Ooey Gooey

Ooey Gooey was a worm,
A wondrous worm was he,
He stepped upon a railroad track,
A train he did not see –
Ooey! Gooey!

Anon

The poor hippopotamus

Consider the poor hippopotamus,
His life is unduly monotonous;
He lives half asleep
At the edge of the deep
And his face is as big as his bottom is.

Anon

On mules we find two legs behind

On mules we find two legs behind
And two we find before.
We stand behind before we find
What those behind be for.
We find before the two before
Just what they, too, be for.
So stand before the two behind
And behind the two before.

Anon

Mary had a little lamb

Mary had a little lamb,
A lobster and some prunes,
A glass of milk, a piece of pie,
And then some macaroons;
It made the naughty waiters grin
To see her order so
And when they carried Mary out,
Her face was white as snow.

Anon

The old person from Fratton

There was an old person from Fratton
Who would go to church with his hat on;
"If I wake up," he said,
"With a hat on my head,
I will know that it hasn't been sat on."

Anon

Down in the river

Down in the river where the lily pods flower,
And the dragonflies buzz by with the bees,
Lives a small mottled frog on the back of a log,
With silver bells strapped to his knees.

As the neatest of tricks, he throws his drum sticks,
Plays a tune on his flute made of reed,
Strums a tiny banjo with a knobbly green toe,
And keeps rhythm with a keyboard of weed.
Then he lets out a scream
As he floats down the stream,
Past the sign: "QUIET PLEASE—
NOISE DISTURBS FROGS."

Sarah Mills

Index of first lines and authors